SMALL-SCALE TEXTILES

YARN PREPARATION

Other books in this series:

Spinning
Dyeing and printing

SMALL-SCALE TEXTILES

YARN PREPARATION

A handbook

John A. Iredale

Intermediate Technology Publications 1992

Practical Action Publishing Ltd
27a Albert Street, Rugby, CV21 2SG, Warwickshire, UK
www.practicalactionpublishing.org

© Intermediate Technology Publications, 1992

First published 1992\Digitised 2013

ISBN 10: 1 85339 042 9
ISBN 13: 9781853390425
ISBN Library Ebook: 9781780443942
Book DOI: http://dx.doi.org/10.3362/9781780443942

All rights reserved. No part of this publication may be reprinted or reproduced or utilized in any form or by any electronic, mechanical, or other means, now known or hereafter invented, including photocopying and recording, or in any information storage or retrieval system, without the written permission of the publishers.

A catalogue record for this book is available from the British Library.

The authors, contributors and/or editors have asserted their rights under the Copyright Designs and Patents Act 1988 to be identified as authors of their respective contributions.

Since 1974, Practical Action Publishing has published and disseminated books and information in support of international development work throughout the world. Practical Action Publishing is a trading name of Practical Action Publishing Ltd (Company Reg. No. 1159018), the wholly owned publishing company of Practical Action. Practical Action Publishing trades only in support of its parent charity objectives and any profits are covenanted back to Practical Action (Charity Reg. No. 247257, Group VAT Registration No. 880 9924 76).

CONTENTS

		Page
	Acknowledgements	vi
	Foreword	vii
	Preface	viii
Chapter 1	Introduction to yarn preparation	1
Chapter 2	Basic principles	3
Chapter 3	Testing and quality control	21
Chapter 4	Small-scale machinery	23
Chapter 5	Production planning	26
Chapter 6	Suppliers of equipment	29
Chapter 7	Sources of further information	32

APPENDICES

1	Calculations	36
2	Comparison of tex with other count systems	39

ACKNOWLEDGEMENTS

It is impossible to mention all the people who, in the forty years of my association with the textile industry, in production, teaching, and research, have contributed to the knowledge which forms the basis of this handbook. However, for the detailed assistance and guidance which was required to ensure that the format and standards matched those of the other publications in this series I would especially thank John Foulds, a friend and colleague since schooldays. Martin Hardingham, the Textile Programme Manager of ITDG, and a friend of many years through our mutual concern for developing countries, must also be included among those who are due for my thanks.

John Iredale

Illustrations and diagrams: Linda Combi, Tanya Lloyd, Samantha Hardingham, Matthew Whitton and Mike Calvert.

FOREWORD

This handbook is one of a series dealing with small-scale textile production, from raw materials to finished products. Each handbook sets out to give some of the options available to existing or potential producers, where their aims could be to create employment or sustain existing textile production, the ultimate goal being to generate income for the rural poor in developing countries. Needless to say, this slim volume does not pretend to be comprehensive. It is intended as an introduction to the topic which may stimulate further enquiry. Although each handbook is complete in itself and provides useful reference material on each specific area of production, the series, taken as a whole, reveals the breadth of technology required to equip a small-scale textile industry. While being primarily technical, the series also covers some of the socio-economic, managerial, and marketing issues relevant to textile production in the rural areas of developing countries.

Production of this series of books has been sponsored by the Intermediate Technology Development Group (ITDG), as part of its efforts to help co-ordinate the most appropriate solutions of particular development problems. The series forms part of the cycle of identifying the need, recognizing the problems, and developing strategies to alleviate the crisis of un- and under-employment in the Third World.

ITDG also offers consultancy and technical enquiry services. For further information write to ITDG. We will be pleased to help.

Martin Hardingham
Textile Programme Manager
ITDG, Rugby, UK

PREFACE

Almost all fabrics, whether woven or knitted, are produced from spun thread. However, this thread or yarn, produced by the spinning operation, either by a hand spinner using the simplest drop spindle or spinning wheel, or spun on the latest automated spinning frame, is rarely in a form suitable to be used immediately for producing a fabric. A broad range of tasks must be undertaken before the actual fabric production operation is reached.

The operations described in this handbook are those which will need to be considered when producing a fabric by even the most basic of techniques. The use of this information should improve the quality of the end product and thus make a positive contribution to the welfare of those involved in this sector of the textile industry.

This handbook is therefore concerned with the principles and practices of the preparation of yarns which have been spun from staple fibres. The preparation of yarns produced from filament fibres, both silk and synthetic, is outside its scope.

John Iredale

1. INTRODUCTION TO YARN PREPARATION

A single spun yarn is seldom ready for immediate use in the production of a fabric. It is usually necessary for the yarn to be rewound from the spindle or spinning bobbin on to a different type of yarn container or 'package' which is more suitable for making the fabric, and in the majority of cases other operations will also be required. The commonest of these is the folding or doubling operation, which involves twisting together two or more single yarns to form a folded yarn, a process which is described more fully in Chapter 2. The words 'twisting', 'folding' and 'doubling' are interchangeable; their use often depends on local practice.

Illustration 1 shows the main operations through which yarn will pass during preparation. Not all yarn passes through all the processes shown: it depends on whether weaving or knitting is to be used to produce the fabric and also to some extent on the types of fibre used to produce the yarn. Like many other areas of textile production, yarn preparation has seen considerable changes in the past

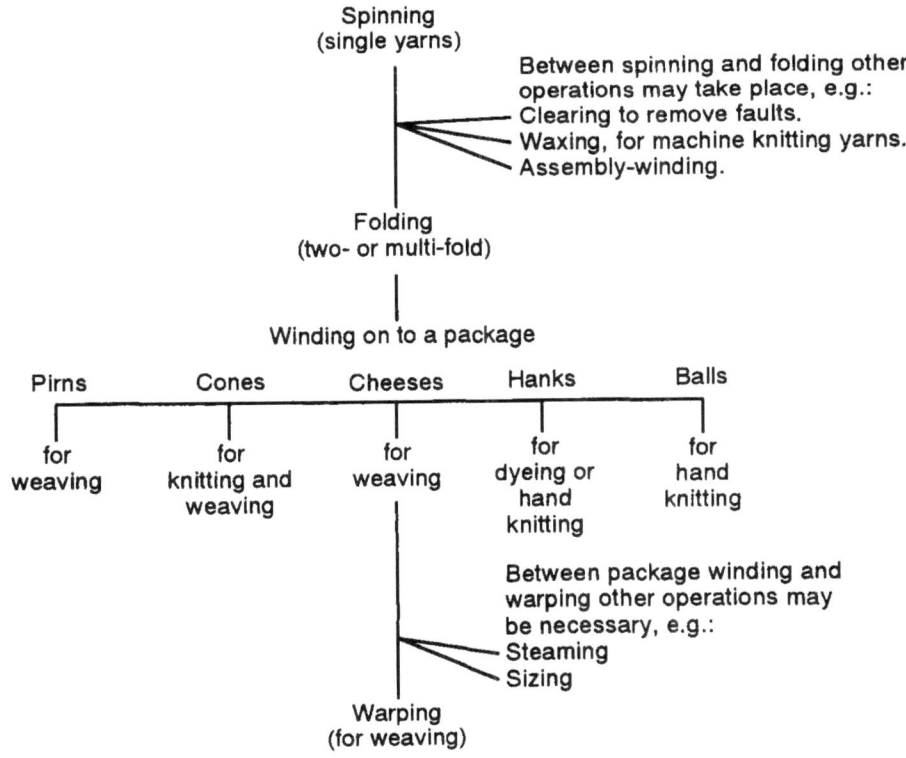

Illustration 1 Stages in yarn preparation

quarter of a century, mostly caused by the rapid increase in knitting as the most popular method of fabric production, and by the increase in use by industry of shuttle-less techniques for weaving.

This handbook will explain those operations which may take place after spinning the yarn and before weaving or knitting the fabric. These operations are very important in producing a good quality product, and as such must be undertaken carefully.

2. BASIC PRINCIPLES

FOLDING, DOUBLING AND TWISTING

After the spinning operation, all yarns will contain accidental thick and thin places. The thin places are usually weaker, which may cause the yarn to break during weaving or knitting. To overcome this problem it is normal to twist together two single yarns (usually described as 'ends'), thus forming a two-fold yarn. Most yarns are used in a two-fold form, although for some products single yarns may be used, for example yarns used in absorbent fabrics for towels, bandages and fine knitwear. For special purposes, such as for carpets and hand-knitting, the yarns may have three, four or even more ends folded or twisted together. These are known as 3-ply or 4-ply yarns, or sometimes as three-fold or four-fold. Yarns with more than three ends are often described as multi-fold yarns. The operation of producing all these yarns can be described as folding, doubling or twisting.

As well as having improved strength and uniformity a folded yarn has much less tendency to snarl, i.e. twist on itself (see Illustration 2), and it is therefore much easier to use in other operations.

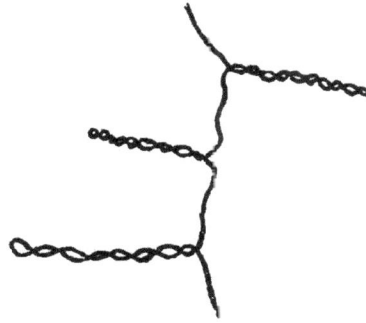

Illustration 2 A yarn which has not been folded has a tendency to snarl

Yarns are folded together with the opposite twist to that used in the spinning process. It is normal to use Z-twist in spinning. S-twist is usually used in the twisting operation, which is achieved by ensuring that the spindle rotates in a clockwise direction (see Illustration 3).

Illustration 3 Z-twist is normally used in spinning; S-twist in folding

The basic aim of the folding process is to combine together equal lengths of single yarn with a uniform amount of twist throughout. This seems a simple thing to do, but if it is not achieved correctly, serious faults may occur later which may be clearly seen in the fabric.

Amounts of twist

The amount of twist inserted in the folding operation is mostly dependent upon the use for which the yarn is intended. The type of end product also influences the amount of twist used to spin yarns and it is often convenient to relate folding twist to spinning twist, whilst spinning twist itself is related to the count or thickness of the spun yarn.

It is usually the case that the twist inserted in the folding operation is such as to give a 'balanced yarn', that is one that will not snarl when it is held in a loose loop (Illustration 4).

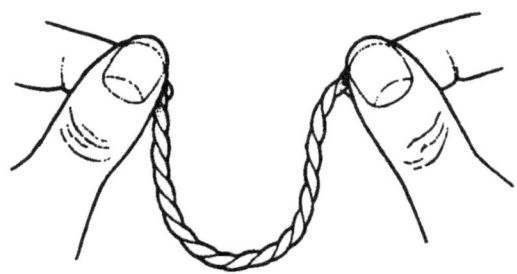

Illustration 4 A balanced folded yarn

There is no general rule which can be applied to say how much folding twist should be used. It is recommended that any yarn should be produced with a balanced twist and if required the twist can be increased to make a harder yarn or decreased to make a softer yarn.

Folded yarn counts

When single yarns are folded together the resultant count of the folded yarn is shown in the following examples:

2 single 40s yarn folded together would be described as two-fold 40s or 2/40s.
3 single 6s yarn folded together would be described as three-fold 6s or 3/6s.

Multi-fold yarns

A wide range of yarns with different properties can be made to meet various needs, by using different combinations of single and folding twists. It therefore follows that this range can be extended by producing three- or multi-fold yarns, although these are generally used only in certain products such as carpets, hand-knitting yarns and cords, or to produce unusual effects in fabrics.

One multi-fold yarn which is popular for hand-knitting is a cable yarn. Such a yarn is made by twisting together two or more yarns which have been already folded. Thus two ends of a two-fold yarn may be twisted together to make a two-fold, two-fold yarn (see Illustration 5). For example, this might be described as 2/2/12s. The direction of twist used in the second folding operation is opposite to that used in the first and the amount is such as to make a balanced yarn (see Illustration 4). The number of component yarns can vary.

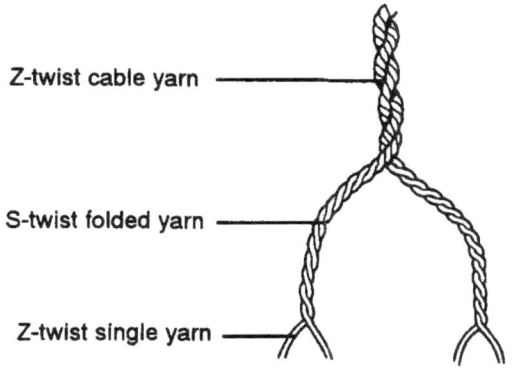

Illustration 5 A two-fold, two-fold yarn

Because cable yarns require additional twisting operations, production costs will increase.

The importance of care in making folded yarns cannot be over-emphasized; any variation in tension in the individual yarns fed into the twisting machine will influence the appearance of the end product. Similarly, when folding different coloured yarns it is essential to handle and arrange the yarns in exactly the same way. Illustration 6 shows the effect of a two-fold yarn made up of black and white components which have been folded with unequal tension. Such a yarn may normally be considered faulty, though sometimes it may be produced deliberately as a fancy yarn, known as a spiral yarn.

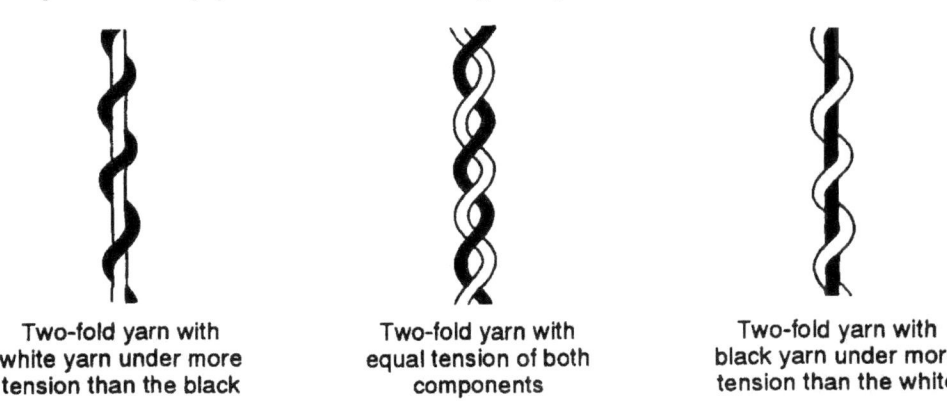

Two-fold yarn with white yarn under more tension than the black

Two-fold yarn with equal tension of both components

Two-fold yarn with black yarn under more tension than the white

Illustration 6 The effect of varying tension in folded yarns

Fancy yarns

Fancy yarns are also produced by twisting or folding. They are used for decorating fabrics or for giving fabrics a novel and unusual structure. Single, two-fold and multi-fold yarns may be combined in various ways, incorporating wool, cotton, silk and any of the synthetic fibres. Fancy yarns include loop, spiral, gimp, cloud, knop, eccentric, stripe, slub and snarl yarns of different types (see Illustration 7).

Some fancy yarns can be made on conventional folding machinery, others require modifications to existing machines, and special twisting machines are necessary for the more complicated ones. Fancy yarns are much more expensive to produce than simple folded yarns because their preparation usually requires at least one extra twisting operation. Further description of their production is outside the scope of this handbook.

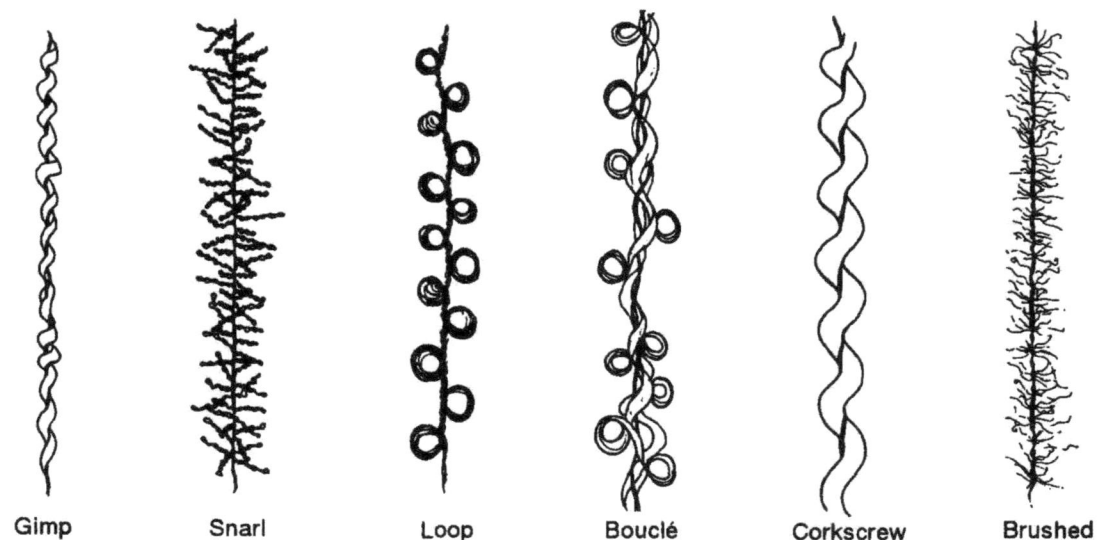

Illustration 7 Some fancy yarns

FOLDING OR DOUBLING EQUIPMENT

It is important to ensure that folding is done in a uniform manner and it is essential that uniform amounts of twist and lengths of yarn are achieved.

The spinning wheel or Indian charkha are the simplest types of equipment on which yarns can be twisted. In many parts of the world any hand- or foot-operated wheel can be used for folding yarns for small-scale production, and the quality of yarn produced is dependent upon the skill of the person using the equipment.

The most common method of folding yarns is by using the ring spindle which is widely used for both spinning and folding. The package is placed firmly on the spindle and rotates with it, driven by a tape (Illustration 8).

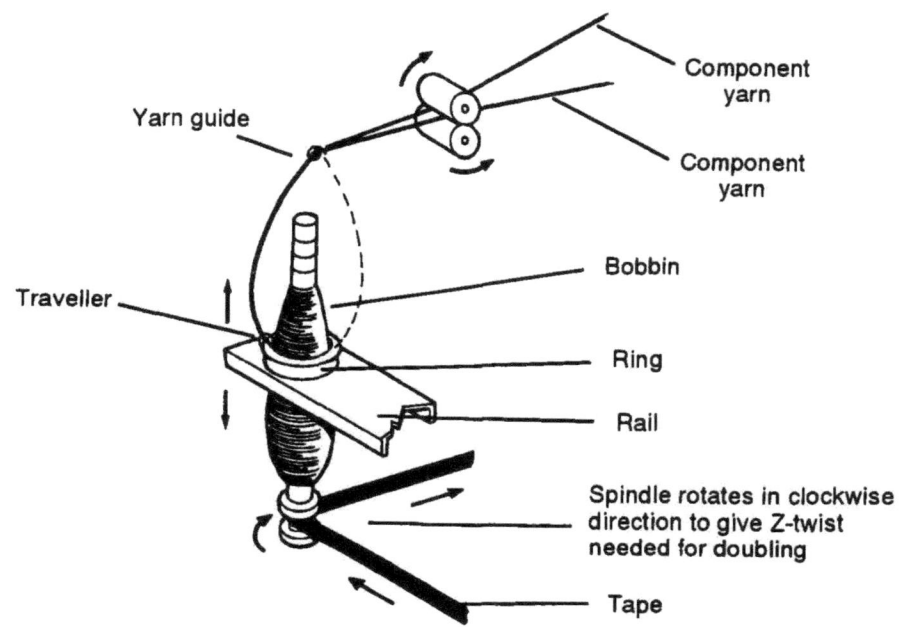

Illustration 8 The most common method of folding yarns is by using a ring spindle

Surrounding each spindle is a flanged metal ring fastened to a rail, which moves up and down to spread the yarn on the package. On the upper flange of each ring there is a small metal clip, called a 'traveller', which is free to rotate around the ring. The yarn coming from the front rollers is threaded through this traveller and fastened to the bobbin. The yarn is wound on to the package because the traveller lags behind the rotation of the spindle and bobbin, causing the yarn to 'balloon' as it is wound on. The traveller guides the yarn on to the bobbin, as the ring and traveller move up and down.

An approximation of twist may be obtained by using the following formula:

$$\text{Turns per inch (tpi)} = \frac{\text{Revolutions per minute of spindle}}{\text{Front roller delivery (inches per minute)}}$$

A more accurate calculation is:

$$\text{Turns per inch} = \frac{\left(\text{Revolutions per minute of spindle} - \frac{\text{Front roller delivery (inches per minute)}}{\text{Package circumference (inches per minute)}}\right)}{\text{Front roller delivery (inches per minute)}}$$

This means that the twist inserted into the folded yarn varies from the inside to the outside of the package as the package circumference varies. Provided that the difference between these two circumferences is kept as small as possible, the difference in twist is such as will not be noticed in the fabric. All ring-twisting packages must therefore be long and thin, rather than short and fat.

Two-fold twisting

This is the commonest method of folding, usually including a ring and traveller, but other methods could be used. Wherever possible this machine should include some form of mechanism which will be triggered if one of the two component threads is missing and will then stop that spindle. This may be achieved by each thread passing through a detector which stops the spindle if that thread breaks.

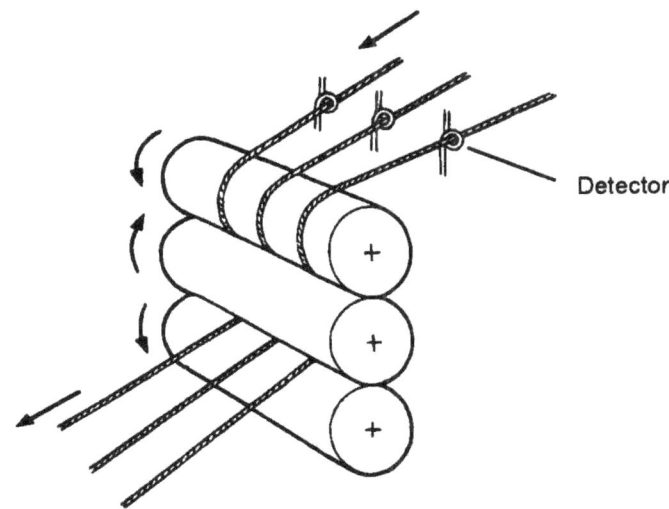

Illustration 9 Feed rollers for multi-folding

Multi-folding

A ring twisting frame is now always used. It consists essentially of a creel for the supply bobbins, a yarn tensioning arrangement, a set of delivery rollers, and spindles.

In some cases the creel may have facilities to carry up to six feeding bobbins per spindle, and each of the single ends is passed through, and arranged to hold up, a detector. The component threads are then passed forward through the feed rollers. It is of particular importance that a uniform rate of feed is maintained and this may be obtained by the use of three feed rollers, usually one above the other (Illustration 9). The detectors are usually located behind the feed rollers. If one of the single ends breaks during the twisting operation, the detector falls, stopping the feed rollers and the spindle. These movements are very quick and leave a sufficient length of yarn behind the rollers to allow broken yarn to be re-tied. This means that if a single yarn breaks and is re-tied, only a single knot appears in the folded yarn rather than one big knot which includes all the yarns.

Stage twisting

This is sometimes known as two-stage twisting, but it can involve more than two operations. It is used in the manufacture of high quality yarns.

The first stage is to combine together, on a package, the number of single yarns needed to make the folded yarn. It is important at this stage of the operation to make certain that the single yarns are fed forward carefully, under equal tension, and thus to ensure that the correct lengths of yarn are combined. These single ends are held together with a small amount of twist (e.g. one turn per inch) as they are wound together on to a large package, thus giving greater lengths of material. This may be described as 'assembly-winding'.

The second stage is to take these combined yarns, held together with the small amounts of twist, and then insert the amount of folding twist finally required. The spindle containing the package prepared at the first stage is now rotated, and the folded yarn is wound on to a suitable package placed above the spindle.

To further improve the quality of yarn, this stage is sometimes preceded by an additional yarn-clearing operation which is described later. The yarn produced by this method is of a higher quality and will thus command a higher price. Such yarns are needed, for example, by machine-knitters where long lengths of 'knotless' yarn (i.e. no knots in the folded threads) are highly desirable.

Two-for-one twisting

As the name suggests, two turns of twist are inserted into the yarn for only one revolution of the twisting spindle. This is achieved by causing the yarn to pass the supply package twice during its route to the take-up package.

Although this method allows twist to be inserted at a higher speed, the package holding the yarn for twisting must first be prepared with the two (or more) yarns wound side by side. This is a separate operation and is known as 'assembly winding', described above.

As with stage twisting, it is often convenient to rewind the yarn from the spinning package on to a cone or 'cheese' before assembly winding and clear the yarn of faults at the same time. This produces greater lengths which contain knots only in the single yarn. This twisting operation may become a three-stage process, as shown in Illustration 10.

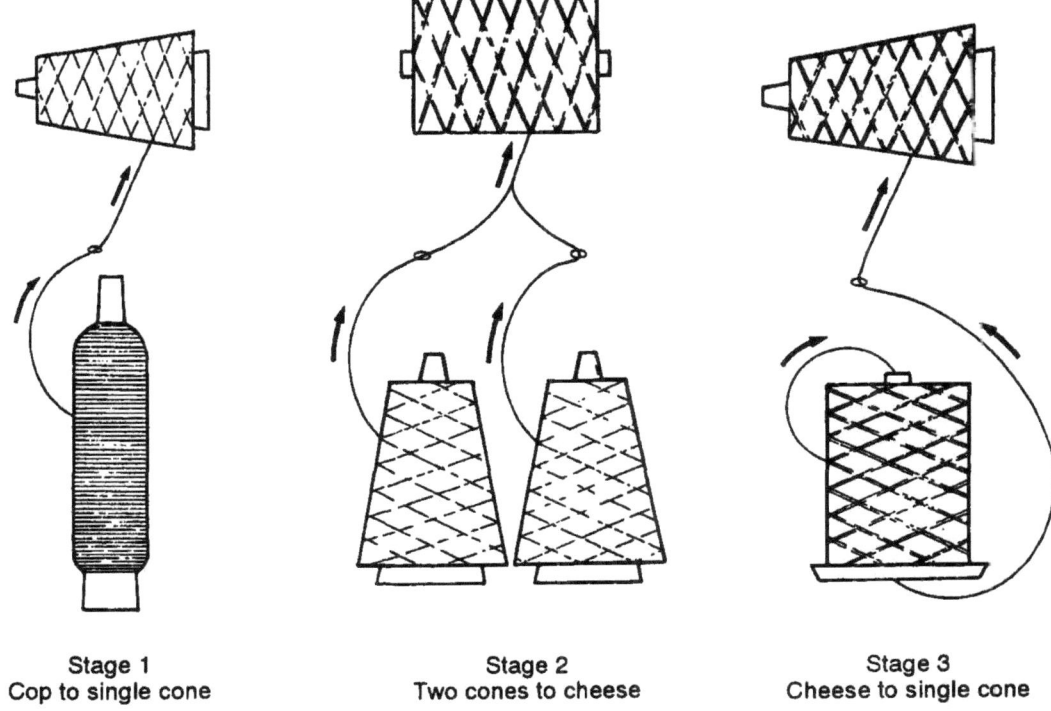

Illustration 10 Two-for-one twisting may be a three-stage process

ADDITIONAL PROCESSES TO IMPROVE YARN PROPERTIES

Clearing

To promote further the uniformity of a folded yarn it is sometimes advantageous to check the spun yarn for irregularities and impurities before the folding operation. This is known as 'clearing'. In this operation the single yarn is usually wound on to a cone, and as it passes from the spinning package to the cone it travels through a fault detector. Simple detectors are mechanical and will identify only large faults or thick places in the spun yarn. If such a fault is detected the yarn is broken by the machine. The operator must then rejoin the broken ends with a special knot, usually a weaver's knot (Illustration 11). This type of knot is used because it lies flat in the fabric.

Illustration 11 A weaver's knot

In clearing, two things may be achieved: not only the removal of faults in the single yarn, but also winding the yarn so that larger packages can be wound. The package of yarn produced by the spinning frame is usually fairly small and thus contains a relatively short length of yarn, resulting in additional work for the folding operator; the much larger package of cleared yarn therefore has the advantages of fewer yarn breakages and lower costs.

Waxing

Waxing acts as a yarn lubricant on yarns which are to be used for machine-knitting. It assists the knitting operation when hairy yarns are being used. The operation is usually carried out by passing the folded yarn against a wax disc (Illustration 12) and may be done at the final winding operation. This is done after and not before dyeing.

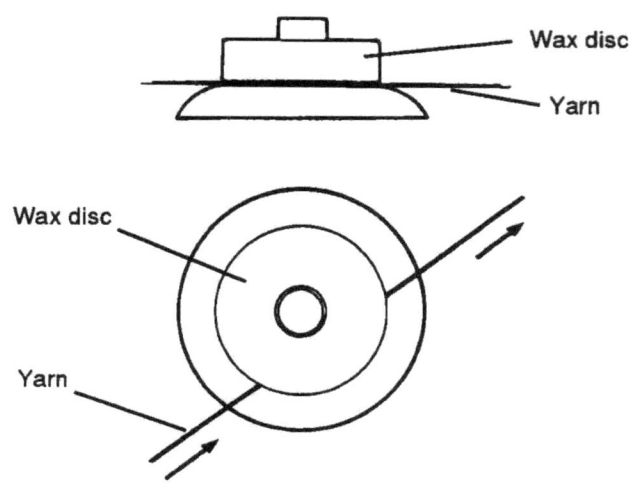

Illustration 12 Waxing the yarn for machine-knitting

Conditioning

It may be important that yarns contain an adequate amount of moisture. To ensure this the yarn can be passed over a roller running in a trough of water at the final winding operation. The amount of water absorbed is difficult to control accurately, but can be influenced by the speed of the conditioning roller, the direction of rotation, and the depth of water in the bath (Illustration 13). Simpler methods of applying moisture can be used but, however simple the method, the application must be uniform.

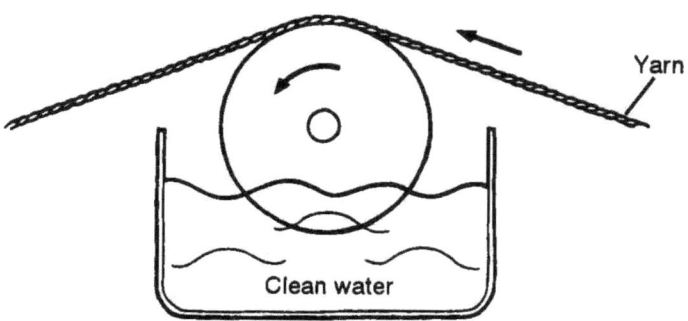

Illustration 13 Conditioning the yarn

Steaming

For making certain hard-wearing fabrics it is desirable that high-twist yarns are used. This makes the yarn very 'twist lively' with a strong tendency to snarl. One way of overcoming this problem is to steam the yarn. To make this easier the folded yarn may be wound on to a perforated cone (Illustration 14). In well-equipped factories, the steaming operation will be done under pressure. In less sophisticated circumstances, simple steaming methods are adequate.

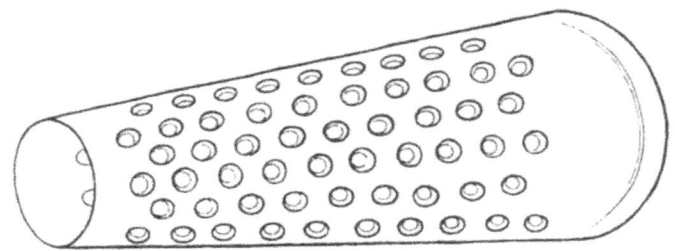

Illustration 14 Perforated cone for steaming the yarn

PACKAGE WINDING

'Winding' is the term used for preparing a package of yarn for the fabric-making process. The yarn can be supplied on different forms of package to the weaver or knitter including spinning and twisting spools, bobbins and tubes, pirns, cheeses and cones, hanks and beams (Illustration 15).

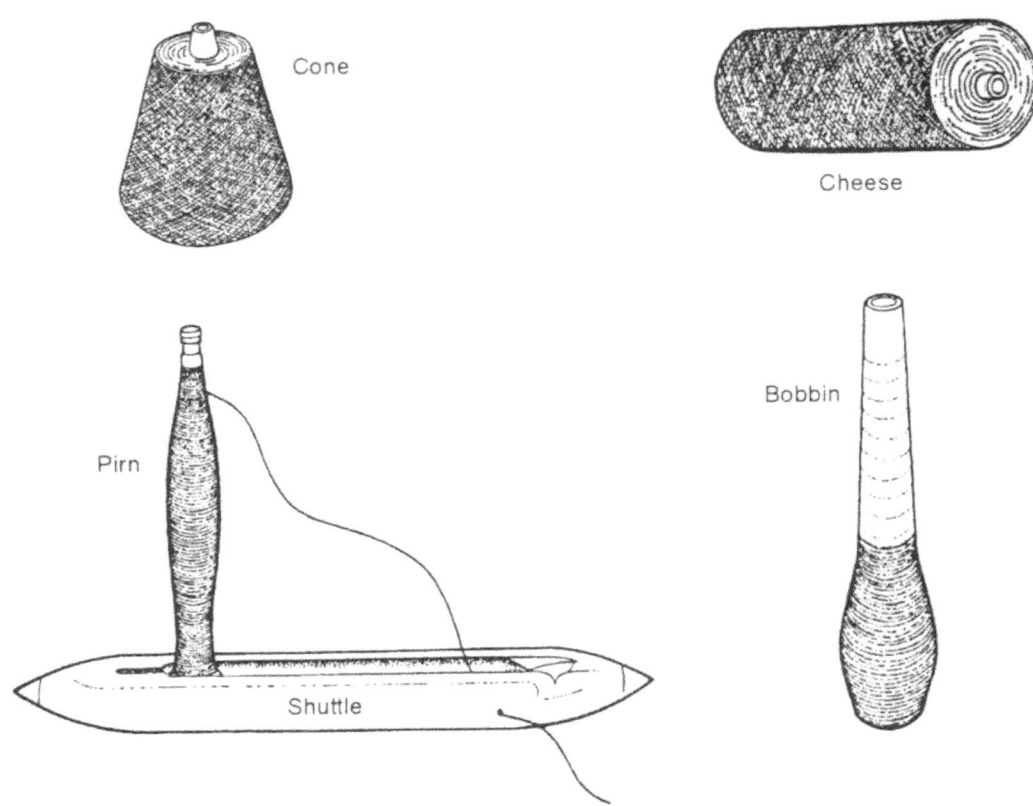

Illustration 15 Different types of package

Cheeses

Cheeses are packages of yarn wound on to parallel wooden, plastic or paper tubes. A lot of yarn can be wound on to cheeses, which is an advantage when making warps. Each cheese will contain 1-2lb (0.5-1.0kg) of yarn, or even more, with a length of up to 22,000 yards (20km) according to the counts. Yarn is unwound from the side of the cheese by allowing the cheese to rotate freely.

Cones

Cones are packages of yarn wound on to conical paper, plastic or wooden tubes and the yarn therefore retains a conical formation. Single and folded yarns for the knitting industry are usually ordered on cones, as this shape of package allows the yarn to be unwound over the narrow end of the cone more easily and with less risk of breaking than on cheeses. On shuttle-less looms, the weft is delivered from a cone.

Pirns

Pirns are wound with weft yarns and inserted into the shuttle for weaving on traditional looms. The pirn must be small enough to fit into the shuttle. However, many modern looms do not use shuttles, and in these cases it is unnecessary to wind the weft on to pirns.

Important points in package winding

The operation of winding a package suitable for the next stage in fabric production can be done by using hand- or power-driven equipment. The equipment may have any number of spindles: for example it is not uncommon to find hand-operated pirn winders having only one, two or four spindles (Illustration 16), whereas in the case of power-driven machines some may have quite large numbers grouped in units of 10-20.

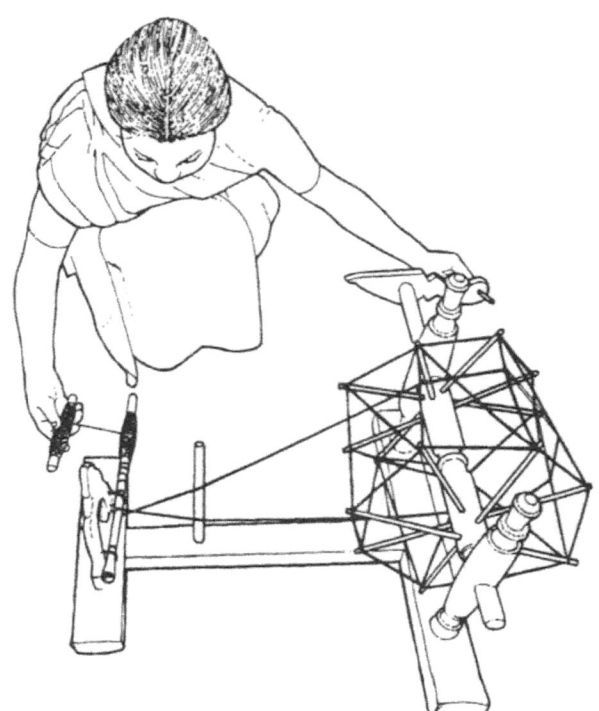

Illustration 16 Hand-operated, single-spindle pirn winder

It is most important that the winding tension is kept uniform, which is often almost impossible to achieve on hand-operated winders. Powered units have not only the advantage of very much higher rates of production, but they also produce a better quality end product.

Large packages are generally desirable to reduce costs and it is not uncommon to find a single cone containing the yarn from as many as 50 spinning bobbins. In the case of pirn winding, the size of the pirn is controlled by the size of the shuttle in which it is to be used.

When a package is being prepared, care must be taken to ensure that the yarn is not damaged. Where clearing takes place the winding operation is likely to improve the quality of the yarn. The yarn must be wound so that it unwinds easily but the package must be firm enough to be handled without damage.

There are two methods of turning the package during winding:

1. a positive drive to the spindle of the package being wound, as in the case of bobbin winding (e.g. using a spinning wheel or charkha, Illustration 17);
2. a friction drive to the surface of the package being wound, as used for cone or cheese winding (Illustration 18).

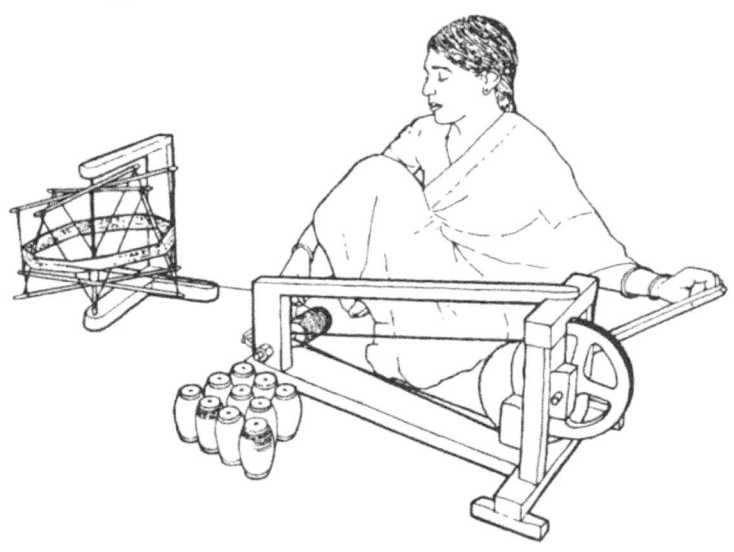

Illustration 17 Hand-operated bobbin winder using positive drive

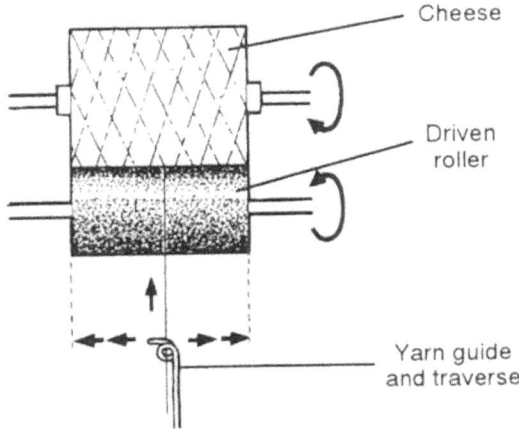

Illustration 18 Cheese winding using friction drive

Where the drive to the spindle is positive a problem may develop in that, as the package size increases, the winding-on speed will also increase, causing changes in yarn tension from the inside to the outside of the package. In the case of a large cheese this change can be very significant. This could be overcome by having a variable speed to the spindle, but that would be complicated. It is more convenient to have a friction drive to the winding package, which gives a constant winding-on speed.

The yarn must be guided on to the package. Some methods guide the yarn to an individual spindle and some guide the yarns to a series of spindles which work in unison. One of the most common methods is to use a split drum or grooved roller which acts as the source of both the friction drive and the guide mechanism (Illustration 19).

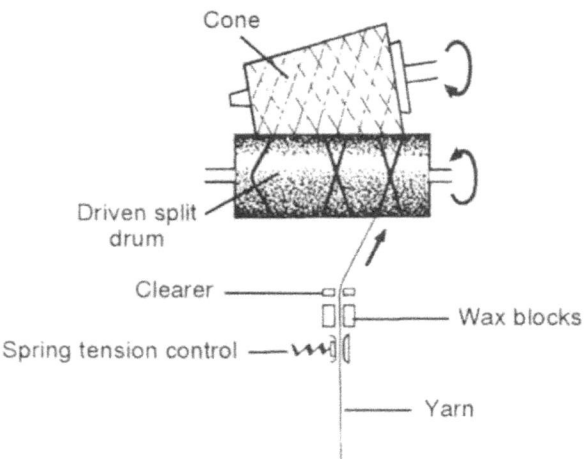

Illustration 19 Cone winding using a split drum

Control of winding packages by hand is difficult. The control of winding tension is important. If it is too low, a soft and unstable package will result; if it is too high, there is a chance of distorting or damaging the yarn. In both cases unwinding will be difficult. The worst condition is where the tension varies throughout the package. To reduce this, some form of tensioning device is usually incorporated in the winding machine. The tension may be controlled by passing the yarn around a series of rods or through a unit where the tension can be increased by the addition of small weights. Yarn tension in the winding process must not vary.

Hank winding or reeling

The oldest and simplest way of making a hank of yarn is by the use of a hand reel or, as it is sometimes known, the 'niddy-noddy' (Illustration 20). This is a simple hand-held device which can be used to wind the yarn, single or folded, into a hank. The yarn should be unwound from the side of the package by rotating it on a peg. Unwinding the yarn over the end of the package should be avoided as this will cause a change in the twist content of the yarn (see Illustration 21). The hank can be made any convenient size.

To wind more than one hank, a reel is used which consists of horizontal wood or metal bars, supported by spokes and connected to a shaft running the full length of the reel (Illustration 22). This is collapsible to allow the hanks to be

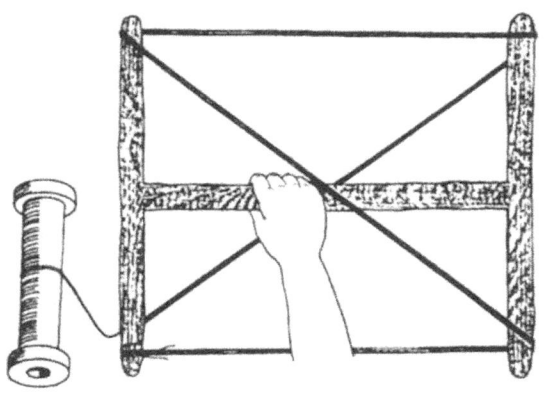
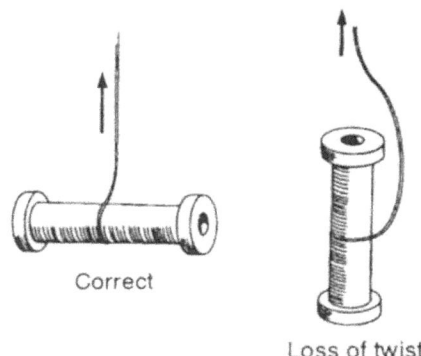

Illustration 20 A niddy-noddy *Illustration 21 The yarn should be unwound from the side of the package*

easily removed. The hanks are taken off by collapsing the reel and removing them over one end. The reel may be fitted with a traversing guide for each hank. Where fine yarns are being wound, a traverse of 2-3 inches (50-75mm) is used to avoid difficulties when rewinding the hank.

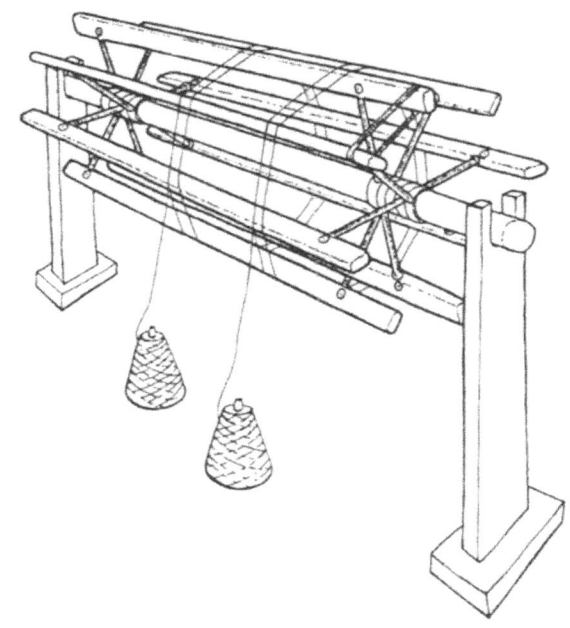

Illustration 22 Equipment for winding more than one hank of yarn

When hanks have been wound, the ends are carefully tied. One or more threads should be interlaced through each hank to avoid entanglement of the yarns during any subsequent scouring or dyeing.

Hanks are used for two purposes: for the hand-knitter and for dyeing.

Reeling is a labour-intensive operation, and the hank is not a very convenient form for modern yarn processing. In many developing countries it is quite common to manufacture and sell yarn in the form of hanks which are combined into bundles, usually containing about 10lb (4-5kg) of yarn.

Warping

A fabric woven on a loom is made up of two separate sets of threads: the warp and the weft. The warp consists of a number of separate threads or 'ends' which run the length of the fabric; the weft is continuous yarn which interlaces the warp to form the fabric (Illustration 23).

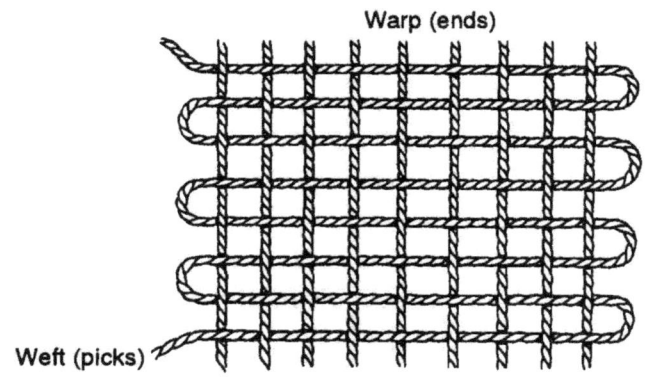

Illustration 23 Warped weft

Warping is the preparation of a number of threads which are arranged in order, number and width, parallel to each other on a beam ready for the loom.

The oldest and simplest way of making a short warp is to use a series of pegs which may be placed on floor, wall or frame, or even on the ground (see Illustrations 24 a and b). The threads must be carefully kept in the correct order. The threads at one or both ends are crossed to form a lease, using extra pegs at each end. The purpose of the lease is to separate the ends so that each thread can be more easily fed into the healds and reed of the loom. The warping frame is best used to prepare a short warp of a small number of ends but it is possible to prepare several narrow warps and place them side by side on a weaving beam, thus building up a wider warp.

Illustration 24a Stick warping with hand-held creel

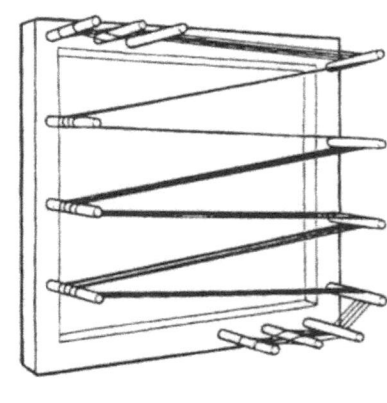

Illustration 24b Frame warping

In the past, vertical warping mills were used; now horizontal warping mills are popular. There are several types of machine available, but in the main they all work on the same principle (Illustration 25). The warp is rewound from the warping mill on to a beam which fits behind the loom.

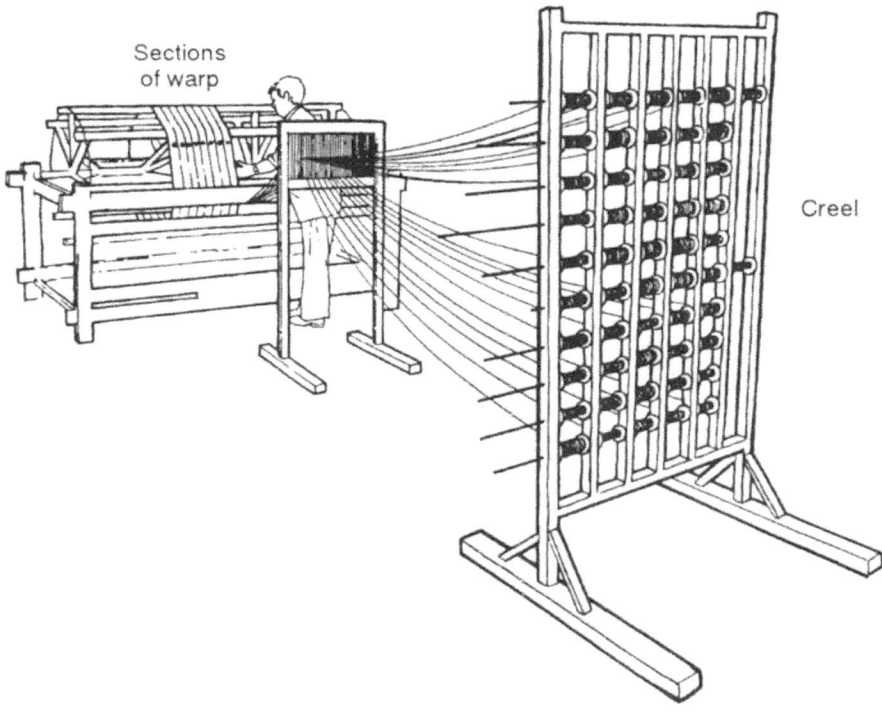

Illustration 25 Horizontal warping mill and upright creel

It is not uncommon for a warp, depending on the type of fabric being woven, to contain several thousands of ends. This warp could be made by using one cone of yarn for each end in the warp. Such an operation would be difficult to control. The normal practice, therefore, is to build up the warp in sections. For example, a warp containing 3300 ends may be made from a creel containing only 220 cones:

$$\frac{3300 \text{ ends}}{220 \text{ cones}} = 15 \text{ sections}$$

This means that the warp will be built up of 15 sections. The situation will not always be as simple as this, particularly in cases where the warp contains a wide range of colours. A further factor which must be considered is the density of the warp threads across the fabric, often referred to as the 'ends per inch' or 'ends per centimetre'. A calculation can be made to determine the width of the warping mill to be occupied by each section. For example, if the total warp of 3300 ends is to be 165cm wide to fit the loom then each section should cover 11cm of the warping mill.

$$\frac{165}{15} = 11 \text{cm}$$

The ends or threads forming the warp pass from the creel after being correctly and uniformly tensioned. They first pass through the dents of a reed, that is through the slots of a special framework, the function of which is to position each thread in order across the warp. It is usual that alternate threads are identified. This is of great importance in all warps but much more so if different colours are used. This identification of threads is known as 'leasing'. The lease can be formed in various ways, the simplest being to pass a thread in front of the reed alternately over and under each thread in the warp. The lease must be retained until the fabric is woven.

The warp threads then pass through the dents of a second or contracting reed. In this case the purpose is to bring the threads closer together so that they have the correct spacing in the fabric. Reeds giving different spacing of threads are available and the correct one must be selected. For example, the warp considered earlier had 3300 ends and was 165cm in the loom; if it were decided to put four ends through each dent there would need to be five dents per centimetre on the reed selected:

$$\frac{3300 \text{ ends in warp}}{165\text{cm in loom} \times 4 \text{ ends per dent}} = 5 \text{ dents per centimetre}$$

The number of ends to be threaded through each dent and the number of dents per centimetre to go in the reed can only be judged with experience and will depend upon the fabric to be woven.

The warp ends then pass through a pair of measuring rollers and through an adjustable guide which controls the width of the section, and are then securely fastened to the warping mill itself. The warp threads are drawn from the creel and wound around the warping mill as it is rotated and the section is made. There is usually a device to give a warning or to stop the machine if an end breaks or when the required length has been wound on. For example if 80 metres have to be wound on, and the warping mill is 4 metres in circumference, then the mill must be stopped after 20 revolutions. The threads are then cut and tied so that they will not unwind while later sections of the warp are being made.

Before the next sections of the warp are made, the creel and reeds should all be removed an appropriate distance along the warping mill so that there is no change in the tension to the threads being wound.

When all the sections have been wound on to the mill the whole warp must be rewound on to a weaver's beam, which is the package placed behind the loom to deliver the warp threads for weaving. The process of rewinding the threads from the weaving mill on to the weaver's beam is known as 'beaming off'. During this rewinding operation the warp should be examined and any faults corrected. The beam is then ready for weaving. Care must be taken not the lose the lease.

Sizing of warps

Size is used mostly to strengthen cotton or rayon warps made from single yarns to make them more suitable for weaving.

There is a range of commercially available sizing agents, but size is often made from natural starch derived from sago, maize, tapioca, farina or rice. As the yarn passes through the various parts of the loom, notably the healds and reeds, some friction occurs. To minimize this, a natural fat such as mutton tallow can be added to the size mixture. It may be desirable to add a wetting agent such as soap which will make it easier for the size to penetrate the yarn.

The size may be added manually or by machine. By whatever method it is added, the process must be completed before weaving. The size mixture must be of a type that can be easily removed in the scouring process before bleaching, dyeing or printing.

The quantity of size added to the warp varies according to the yarn being processed. Generally the total amount of size mixture added will vary from 4 per cent to 15 per cent based on the weight of the yarn. If too much size is added, weaving becomes impossible.

Sizing may be carried out on yarns in the form of hanks, or from warp beams, and the equipment required for adding the size will vary.

Hank sizing is a relatively simple operation. The hanks are immersed in the size solution, squeezed dry and hung on poles to dry. It is important, however, that the hanks are prepared using a reel with a traverse mechanism, as otherwise the sized hank will be very difficult to unwind.

It is more usual for the size to be added after the warp has been prepared. The completed warp, if it is not too long, is collected together in the form of a rope, being careful not to lose the lease bands. The rope is then passed through the sizing agent in as loose and open a way as convenient and hung up to dry.

The warp to be sized may first be spread in an open form between two sticks held under tension in a strong framework. The threads are spread evenly across the supporting sticks and lease rods are inserted at intervals to keep the threads in order (Illustration 26). The warp is removed from the frame, rolled, and size is applied with the aid of a brush or cloth by gradually unrolling or re-rolling the warp (Illustration 27).

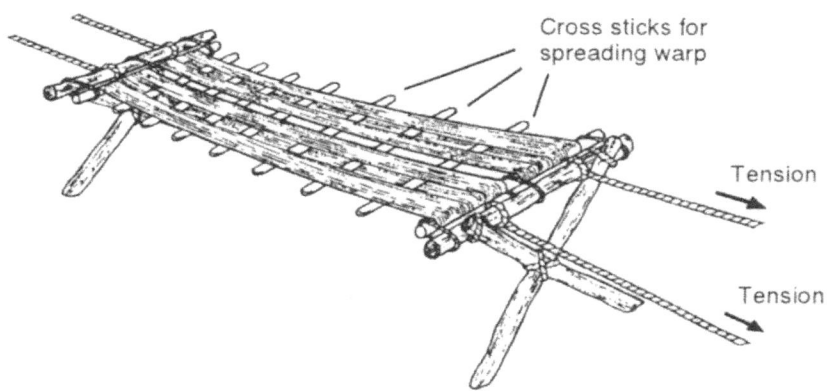

Illustration 26 The warp held under tension for sizing

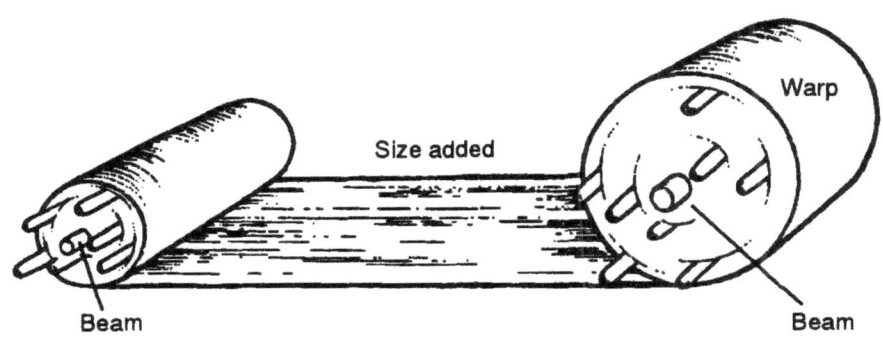

Illustration 27 Warp rolled after sizing

The roll is left to soak for about half an hour and then tensioned in the supporting frame. After re-spreading it is left in a shaded place so that the warp does not dry too quickly. It is brushed frequently, using a wide brush with stiff bristles, turning the warp to treat both sides. This is repeated until the warp is dry and all the threads are separated. If the warp dries too quickly before the threads are separated it can be sprayed lightly with water. Finally, the separating sticks are removed and the warp is ready for winding into a beam.

It cannot be over-stressed that the operations in yarn preparation must be done carefully and accurately if the quality of the fabric, whether knitted or woven, is to be maintained. The whole of this chapter can be summarized in a few words:

care, uniformity, balanced twist, correct package.

3. TESTING AND QUALITY CONTROL

Maintenance of quality in making a product to a previously agreed specification and uniformity is an essential feature of every stage of textile processing, and yarn preparation is no exception. In fact it could be argued that it is one of the more important stages in terms of quality as variations which occur, particularly in the yarn folding and warping operations, are always easily seen in the fabric.

For the purpose of this chapter it must be assumed that the yarn which forms the starting point for yarn preparation is correct. However, it is always a very sensible practice to check this and a manufacturer receiving single yarn from a spinner would be well advised to check the quality of the yarn regularly. Tests of count, i.e. the thickness of the yarn, and the twist in the singles yarn should always be carried out. In some instances such features as strength, colour and the fibre composition of the yarn should also be checked.

Twist-testing of the folded yarn is most important because variations in twist can be seen easily in the woven or knitted fabric. This is because there is a big difference in the appearance of yarns containing different amounts of twist. For example if there is a continuous variation across the fabric, known as a bar, which stands out as being different, it may be caused by a variation in twist. This can be confirmed by viewing the material from each edge or selvage of the fabric. If the bar appears darker from one edge than from the other, then the fault is almost certainly caused by a variation in twist in the yarns. The same problem could arise in the warp, then a darker or lighter stripe would be seen along the length of the fabric for the same reasons.

To prevent this type of fault, twist tests should be carried out on the folded yarn at regular intervals. To do this, a convenient length of yarn, say 10 inches (250mm), is selected and the twist removed, and a note taken of the number of turns of twist contained. At least ten such tests should be carried out and the average twist calculated (see Appendix 1 for calculations). A minimum of ten tests are required to give a result which is reliable. If the result is different from that expected, a further ten tests should be done to confirm the result. This test is most conveniently done using a commercial twist tester (Illustration 28) which, whilst holding one end firm, holds the other in a jaw which will rotate and so untwist the yarn. At the same time a record of the number of turns required to untwist the 10 inches of yarn is recorded on a dial. A more simple twist tester can be made (Illustration 29). It is important that the yarn is tested under constant tension and that all the tests are done in the same way to obtain consistency of result.

One reason for twisting yarns together is to improve their strength, and strength-testing of yarns is sometimes important. This can be done by testing the strength of an individual length of yarn or by testing a series of lengths of yarn, often in the form of a hank. Various commercial machines are available for this. Some comparison of yarn strengths can, however, be obtained by making a hank of yarn containing a known number of threads and then suspending the hank from a convenient bar or hook and hanging a series of weights on it until it breaks. This is not an accurate method but will enable comparisons between yarns to be made. When yarns are tested for strength in this way it is important that the new yarn is tested at the same time as the one with which it is being compared. Most fibres and yarns are influenced by moisture conditions in the atmosphere, and big differences in strength can be observed which are sometimes only caused by the moisture content of the yarn. This fact is well known, for instance, to many people who are already familiar with the differences in strength between wet rope and dry rope. It should be noted also that different fibres behave differently when they contain different amounts of moisture: some become stronger, some become weaker.

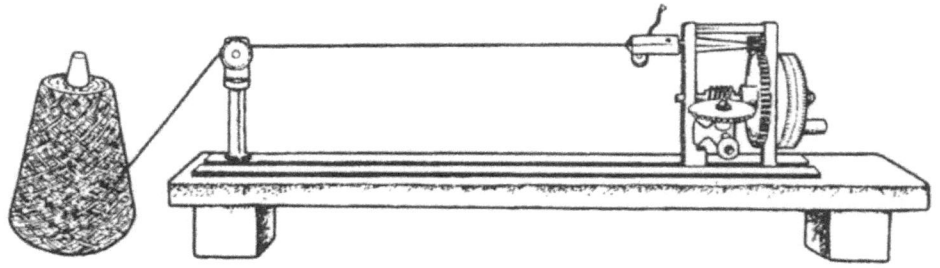

Illustration 28 Commercial twist testing apparatus

Illustration 29 Simple twist tester

It is also important that the preparation of the warp is correct. There is no special equipment for this; it is really a matter of checking the arrangements of the threads by eye. This is sometimes a lengthy task but it is much better to do it before weaving and thus avoid making a faulty piece of fabric. The most difficult warp to check is one containing a large number of different coloured ends, perhaps intended to make a striped piece of cloth. Sometimes the whole warp is examined in an operation known as warp-dressing, but more usually only such factors as the length of the warp, the number of ends per inch and the arrangements of coloured ends etc. are the characteristics checked.

Textile testing is, in a commercial environment, a very complex process often done by automatic machines, thus avoiding human error. The test results will be considered mathematically, perhaps even using a computer. If only simple testing equipment is available and accurate results are required an alternative is to send the yarn to a testing laboratory.

4. SMALL-SCALE MACHINERY

This chapter is a brief survey of some small-scale machinery. For yarn preparation it is particularly difficult to give specifications, for several reasons:

1. Some equipment, for example pirn winders, can be very simple and can be made in most village workshops and, in many cases, at home.
2. In practice, many small-scale producers use machinery which has been made from parts of old industrial machinery. The size and complexity of the machine will depend on which parts are available after being discarded by industry.
3. This is the section of the textile manufacturing where it is still not uncommon to find equipment made largely from wood, for example charkhas, reels and warping machines. These can be produced in a village workshop.
4. The output of any hand-operated machinery will vary and is dependent upon many factors from the quality of the yarns being handled to the energy of the user. Therefore it would seem more appropriate to show the methods which can be used to calculate the rate of production at each operation. Examples of production calculations for each operation are shown in Appendix 1.
5. When estimating production levels of equipment used in yarn preparation, it is essential to include in the calculation a figure which shows the time spent when the machine is stopped for creeling, removal of full packages and joining broken ends. This is called the machine efficiency and is expressed as a percentage. Efficiency figures are variable. In a modern textile factory the efficiency of the doubling section could be as high as 90 per cent, with 70 per cent a more normal figure. Levels as low as 40 per cent are not unknown. For hand-operated equipment, when considered over a whole working day, percentages will be even lower.

Production calculations for all the machine examples given are included in Appendix 1.

Hand-operated winding machines

Hand-operated winders may vary from simple modifications of the single-spindle charkha to two- or four-spindle winders. Small power-driven pirn winders are available with up to 12 spindles (Illustration 30).

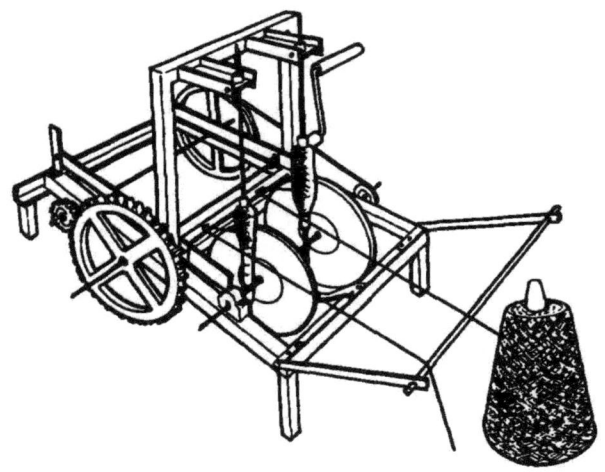
Illustration 30
Hand-operated, double-spindle pirn winder

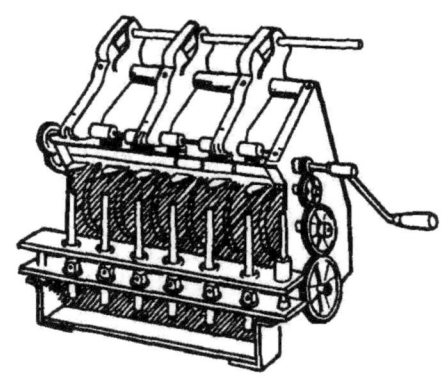
Illustration 31
Hand-operated, six-spindle ring doubler machine

Folding or doubling

Hand-operated four- or six-spindle flier or ring frames are usually used for doubling yarns in small-scale production units (Illustration 31).

Production rates are dependent upon the speed of rotation of the spindle and the number of turns of twist required in the yarn, together with the count of the yarn being processed. Examples are given in Appendix 1 using both cotton and tex count systems.

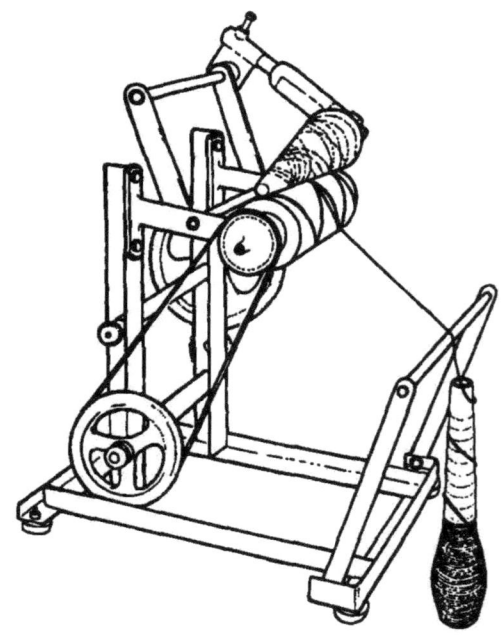
Illustration 32 Hand-operated cone winder

HANK AND PACKAGE (CONE AND CHEESE) WINDING MACHINES

The method of calculating the rate of production in winding will depend on the type of machinery used.

The machinery required for preparing a hank – usually described as reeling – can be as simple as the niddy-noddy shown in Illustration 20 (page 15) which makes only a single hank. Illustration 22 shows a machine in which several hanks can be produced at the same time. Reels can be very simple and can easily be rotated by hand or power.

The winding of packages is more difficult as the yarn must be carefully and accurately guided on to the package. Locally built winders making one or more packages are common and may in some cases be hand driven. Except in the most simple conditions it is usual to use an electric motor to drive the winder; only small amounts of power are required.

WARPING MACHINES

Warping equipment can vary from the simplest form, pegs in the ground or on a frame, to quite complex horizontal warping mills. For small-scale production it will be most probable that, whatever system is used to make the warps, the equipment will be manufactured locally.

The rate of production in the warping section is primarily determined by the type of warping mill and creel which is used. In cases where modern machines are used, up to 80 per cent efficiency may be achieved. This is, however, exceptional and figures in the range of 35-40 per cent are much more normal.

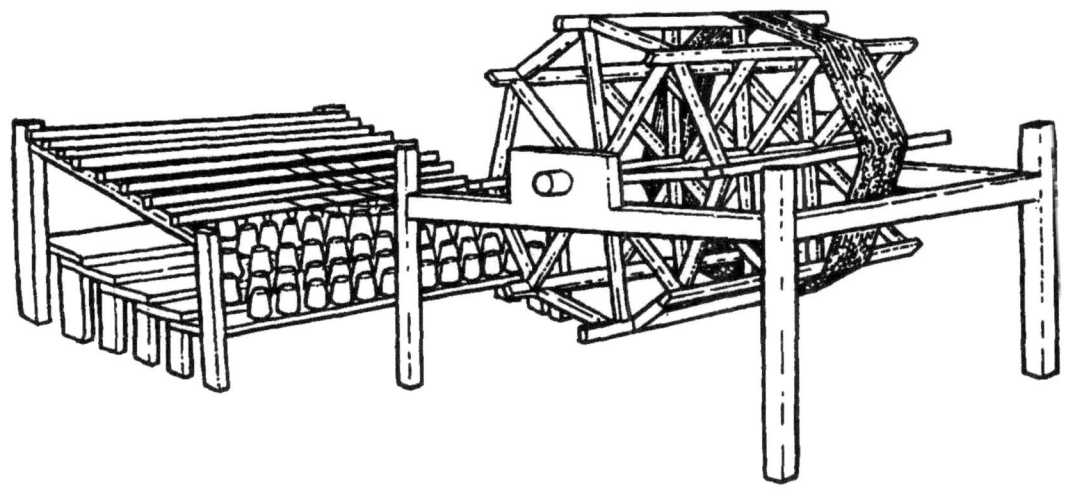

Illustration 33   Small, wooden, hand-operated, sectional warping mill with horizontal step creel

5. PRODUCTION PLANNING

The situations in which yarns are prepared for weaving on simple equipment are likely to vary widely. It may be intended to establish production in a new situation where there is little local experience and knowledge, or perhaps a well-established local activity is to be improved or expanded. Whatever the intention, careful planning is important and a few basic requirements must be met to achieve a successful result.

If preparation is to be organized in a centralized manner, rather than in individual households, the decision must be based upon the type and quantity of material needed to meet a particular known requirement. If yarns have to be supplied from a distance, the availability and cost of transport must be carefully assessed.

The way in which the preparation will be organized locally needs to be considered. The space or building in which production will take place can be arranged in any way that is convenient but it should be dry, light and airy, with good shade. The processing and storage of the raw materials should never be in direct sunlight. The space should be arranged so that materials can be moved easily. The building should include a secure area to store both the basic yarns and the material after preparation. The storage area should be light and have good ventilation. Yarns should be stored off the ground on wooden shelves or slats, and in a way that allows frequent inspection for signs of attack by insects or mildew. All natural textile fibres are subject to such attacks and, in the absence of chemical treatment to prevent attacks, frequent inspection and turning, combined with storage in light and airy conditions out of direct sunlight are the best precautions.

It is unlikely that the working area will be air conditioned, so ideal atmospheric conditions will not always be available. For most processing 50–65 per cent relative humidity at 20°–25°C will be reasonable. Very low humidity will cause most problems and the yarns will be difficult to control. If the atmosphere is very dry some water should always be present in the working area: perhaps some areas of the floor can be sprinkled or containers of water left in several places. High humidity and temperature are an aid to processing, but then there may be problems with mildew attack on any stored materials.

Some waste will occur during preparation from broken yarns; these have some value and should be carefully collected and stored for sale as yarn waste.

The area in which the yarns are received should contain a bench and suitable weighing equipment to check deliveries. It would also be useful to have a small area in which simple yarn testing could take place. Checking the count, that is the thickness of the yarns, the twist, and yarn strength are all useful quality control procedures.

If yarn preparation is being introduced as a new activity to an area, or if a new type of equipment is being recommended, suitable training should be considered an essential first step. With both hand- and power-operated equipment, skill and knowledge of the process will bring dividends in terms of the quality of the end product. If possible some training should be started, even if only for one or two key personnel, before the establishment of a new unit. The training programme should also include discussions with all those who might be involved with the activity. The social problems which may arise from a failure to introduce new ideas successfully and with local agreement can be a major barrier to any new venture. Suitable training is sometimes available at major textile centres or educational institutions in the area and these possibilities should be investigated. Any training programme must also include the safety aspects of using new and perhaps unfamiliar equipment.

BASIC CONDITIONS

Before making any decisions about the scale of equipment needed in a new situation, or before modifying the existing type of equipment, the following points should be carefully considered.

COST Is there sufficient justification for the level of expenditure planned? Is there sufficient cash available to meet purchase costs? If money is borrowed for purchases, can it be repaid satisfactorily? Are there any local or government-supported loan schemes to cover the capital cost of equipment or for the establishment of small industries? Is sufficient cash available to meet day-to-day running expenses, wages, work in progress and purchase of stocks?

CAPACITY Does the choice of equipment match the desired production and the availability of supplies? Is there room for expansion? Is the equipment flexible enough to give some variation in end product?

LOCATION If the equipment and other facilities are located in one place, will this suit all those who expect to use it? Would temporary locations and portable equipment be more suitable? If materials have to be moved between different locations, is suitable transport available at reasonable cost?

AVAILABILITY Is the equipment available locally from a reputable manufacturer? If not, is anyone willing to manufacture or sell the equipment in the district? Is the equipment available locally for hire, loan or share? Are manufacturing instructions available and are there sufficient skills to carry out construction? What kind of spare parts and advisory service are on hand or will be needed? If power-driven equipment is being planned, is a reliable power supply available for a reasonable period each day?

EXPERIENCE Is the equipment easy to use? Can tuition be obtained locally or at a national training centre? What local skills exist, or could be developed, for maintaining and servicing the equipment?

OPERATIVE SKILLS The most important skills required by the operative are those of care and accuracy. Yarn preparation is, by comparison to many other textile processes, very clean and in most cases there are few health or safety hazards. Noise is usually not a problem unless very high-speed winders are being used.

SOCIAL ACCEPTABILITY Will the choice of equipment and system be readily acceptable to local people? What changes to existing social practice will be required? Has the demand for change come from the local community or from outside? After shortlisting the most suitable range of equipment, an economic evaluation of all inputs and outgoings associated with it will help to identify the best technical choice. Finally, before purchase you seek expert advice about the equipment and how you propose to use it.

ECONOMICS OF YARN PRODUCTION

Once an operation has been planned in some detail, it is a useful exercise to undertake a trial costing for the production of packages or warps to give a rough idea of the viability of the operation in commercial terms. The cost of any yarn has two components: overheads (fixed or indirect costs) and variable (direct costs).

Indirect costs

1. Interest on the cost of any stock of raw materials
2. Cost of premises
3. Heat/light/power
4. Telephone
5. Cost of depreciation on equipment and interest on any loans for its purchase
6. Consumable materials
7. Insurance
8. Postage/stationery.

Direct costs

1. Raw materials (single yarns)
2. Wastage (5 per cent for winding, 3 per cent for warping – at the very least)
3. Transport costs
4. Wages (including any contribution to a welfare fund and any incentive wages).

Once an estimate of production has been made for the planned unit, the above costs can be worked out for one week's production. The actual processing costs are then the weekly indirect costs plus the weekly direct costs, divided by the number of product units made per week. To this actual cost must be added any profit per unit (packages or warp beams) to give the final basic selling price.

6. SUPPLIERS OF EQUIPMENT

The details included here are those of small-scale machine manufacturers; those manufacturers who may be sympathetic to the supply of small units, sometimes hand-operated; and those willing to meet special requirements. Makers of large-scale machines are not included.

PIRN-WINDERS

Single-spindle, hand-operated

Frank Herring & Son
    27 Highwest Street
    Dorchester DT1 1UP
    Dorset
    UK

The Handweavers Studio and Gallery Ltd
    29 Haroldstone Road
    London E17 7AN
    UK

Double-spindle, hand-operated

Development Alternatives (TARA)
    22 Olof Palme Marg
    Vasant Vihar
    New Delhi 110 057
    India

Gujarat Khadi Gramodyog Mandal
    Harijan Ashram
    Ahmedabad 38 00 27
    Gujarat
    India

Multi-spindle, power-operated

W. Schlafhorst
    Postfach 205
    4050 Monchengladbach
    Germany

REELS

Gujarat Khadi Gramodyog Mandal
    Harijan Ashram
    Ahmedabad 38 00 27
    Gujarat
    India

HANK WINDERS

Wrap reels for testing purposes

V.P.F. Testing Equipment
    Venkatapathy Foundry
    Peetamedu
    Coimbatore
    S. India

James Heal & Sons Ltd
    Lake View
    Woodside
    Halifax HX3 6EP
    UK

WARPING EQUIPMENT

Hand-operated

Farnham Loom Co.
    Magpie Works
    Station Approach
    Four Marks
    Nr Alton
    Hampshire GU34 5HN
    UK

Handweaving Studio & Gallery Ltd
    29 Haroldstone Road
    London E17 7AN
    UK

Machine-operated

James Mackie & Sons Ltd
    PO Box 149
    Belfast BT12 7ED
    UK

BALLING MACHINE

12- or 16- spindle semi-automatic range of winding machines for specialist purpose

William Ayrton & Co. Ltd
    Gorebrook Works
    Leizsight
    Manchester M12 5RH
    UK

CONE WINDING MACHINES

Hand-operated

Gujarat Khadi Gramodyog Mandal
  Harijan Ashram
  Ahmedabad 38 00 27
  Gujarat
  India

1-12 head power-driven

Thess Textile Machines
  71 Abbey Lane
  Leicester EE4 5QV
  UK

7. SOURCES OF FURTHER INFORMATION

It is quite impossible in a simple volume of this sort to include anything more than the basic outlines of the operations involved in yarn preparation. Although much has been published about the main textile areas of yarn manufacture and fabric production (both weaving and knitting), because yarn preparation tends to be a series of link operations there have been very few books specifically directed to this area of processing. Consequently it may be necessary to extract information, often limited, from volumes which are primarily directed to the other major areas of processing.

An additional problem is that such volumes are usually directed towards the processing of wool or cotton and are not general. Reference to wool or cotton is now a rather dated approach when one considers the vast quantity of synthetic fibres processed. Reference to long and short staple processing may be more correct.

However, some information is available. The volumes which are listed here have all been produced for use by textile technologists working with the latest equipment, which may not always be relevant to developing countries. The books listed are all available, at the time of writing.

The main international professional body for the textile industry is the Textile Institute which among their other services has both a library (available to members) and a book sales department (available to anyone).

Most of the organizations mentioned below are useful sources of information. If detailed information is needed it is often important to know which department or individual to approach. ITDG in Rugby, UK, is often able to give advice or direct enquiries to the appropriate person or department.

1. Research organizations. Many have information services which are available even to non-members.
2. Other useful sources of information including institutions, federations and guilds.
3. Written sources of information. This includes a selected list of publications used in the compilation of this manual.

1. RESEARCH ORGANIZATIONS

(a) They almost always have an information service on a wide range of textile topics. This usually includes book lists and copies of research papers.
(b) They will usually undertake testing or other work for which a charge is made.
(c) They sometimes organize courses or training programmes in aspects of textile manufacture.

United Kingdom

International Wool Secretariat, Technical Centre, Valley Drive, Ilkley, LS29 8PB. Tel 0943 601555. Telex 51457

British Textile Technology Group, Shirley Towers, Didsbury, Manchester, M20 8RX. Tel: 061 445 8141. Fax: 061 434 9957. Tlx: 668417

British Textile Technology Group, Wira House, West Park Ring Road, Leeds, LS16 6QL. Tel: 0532 781381. Fax: 0532 780306. Tlx: 557189

British Textile Technology Group, Newton Business Park, Talbot Road, Hyde, SK14 4UQ. Tel: 061 367 9030. Fax: 061 367 8886

India

The South India Textile Research Association (SITRA) Coimbatore 641014, Tamil Nadu

Ahmedabad Textile Industry Research Association (ATIRA), Polytechnic Post Office, Ahmedabad 380015, Gujarat

Textile and Allied Research Association (TAIRO), Baroda, Gujarat

Training courses in spinning can sometimes be organized at khadi centres by KVIC, Bombay, or directly at the Gandhi Ashram, KG Prayog Samsti, Ahmedabad 380027, Gujarat. Tel: 4/60524

2. OTHER USEFUL SOURCES OF INFORMATION

United Kingdom

The Textile Institute, 10 Blackfriars Street, Manchester M3 5DR
Tel: 061 843 8457. Tlx: 668297

Association of Guilds of Weavers, Spinners and Dyers, BCM 963 London WC1N 3XX

India

Khadi and Village Industries Commission, Irla, Vile Parle, Bombay 400056

Centre for Appropriate Technology, Indian Institute of Technology, Hauz Khas, New Delhi 110016

Rajasthan Small Industries Corp (RAJSICO) 2nd Floor, Udyog Bhawan, Tilak Marg, Jaipur, 302005

Aga Khan Rural Support Programme, Choice Premises Swastik Crossroads, Navrangpura, Ahmedabad 380009, Gujarat

3. PUBLISHED SOURCES OF INFORMATION

Books about textiles which contain information on yarn preparation
(some of these can only be obtained from libraries)

Hall, A. J. *Standard Handbook of Textiles* (Butterworth)

Morton, W. E. and Wray G. R. *An Introduction to the Study of Spinning* (Wira Library)

Shaw C. and Eckersly F. *Cotton* (Pitam)

Atkinson R. R. *Jute* (Temple Press)

Brearley A. and Iredale J. A. *The Woollen Industry* (Wira)

Brearley A. and Iredale J. A. *The Worsted Industry* (Wira)

Books and papers containing more specialized information on yarn preparation

De Barr A. E. and Catling H. *Manual of Cotton Spinning Volume 5* (Textile Institute)

von Bergen W. *Wool Handbook, Volume 2 Part 1* (John Wiley, New York)

Dyson E., Iredale J. A. and Parkin W. *Yarn Preparation and Properties* (Textile Institute)

Paul S. K. *Study in Modern Jute Technology* (Dasgupta, Calcutta)

Wool Science Review, Volumes 6,10,20,33 (International Wool Secretariat)

Happey F. (Ed.) *Contemporary Textile Engineering* (Academic Press)

Books on textile testing

Methods of Test for Textiles (British Standards Institution)

Booth J. E. *Principles of Textile Testing* (National Trade Press)

Development and Transfer of Technology Series, No. 4 (UNIDO Vienna)

Useful published references with specific details on yarn preparation include:

Lord P. R. and Mohammed M. H. *Weaving: Conversion of Yarn to Fabric* (Second Edition, Merrow 1973)

Marks R. and Robinson A.T.C. *Principles of Weaving* (Textile Institute, 1976)

Slater K. *Textile-Mechanics Volume 1* (Textile Institute, 1977)

Booth J.E. *Textile-Mathematics Volume 1-3* (Textile Institute, 1975-77)

Technical information and advice is also available from various research establishments. Most of these organizations operate on a commercial basis, so advice may be limited to those who are members or who are willing to pay for the information they require, but many organizations will give some limited guidance in an informal way. Throughout the world there are several such organizations which have varying levels of expertise.

The Textile Institute and the British Textile Technology Group are the major textile research and consultancy organizations located in the UK. The latter is essentially a research organization whose area of interest covers all textile fibres and processes. In addition to their very wide-ranging research and testing work they operate an international consultancy department. They also manufacture testing equipment, and offer for sale a limited number of their own publications.

There are a considerable number of private consultants, some of whom have many years of industrial experience and are available for international advisory work; such consultants are totally independent. Lists of such consultants are available from The Textile Institute, Manchester, UK.

APPENDIX 1
CALCULATIONS

These calculations are included to further explain the way that production figures etc. can be calculated. In most cases the methods used remain the same whether imperial or metric units (inches or millimetres) are used.

Calculation 1 Twist testing

In Chapter 3, reference was made to the testing of folding twist using a 10-inch (250mm) twist tester. A typical set of results obtained for ten tests could be:

Test no.	Twist
1	153.6
2	149.7
3	152.3
4	161.9
5	148.4
6	157.9
7	159.2
8	161.4
9	155.3
10	156.1

Divide by no. of tests 10 | 1555.8 Total

155.58 Average turns of first 10 inches

Therefore average turns per inch = 15.5

Calculation 2 Productivity in folding or doubling

This is dependent upon two factors:

1. the amount of twist to be put into the folded yarn
2. the thickness, or count of the yarn.

Both these factors can vary greatly, so productivity rates can be very variable. The thickness of a yarn is described by counts and many systems are used; two systems are used in the examples below.

Example 1 Imperial units and cotton count

$$\frac{\text{Spindle speed (revolutions per minute)}}{\text{Number of turns of twist (turns per inch)}} = \text{Number of inches of folded yarn produced}$$

$$\frac{\text{Number of inches of folded yarn produced}}{36} \times \frac{\text{Ply}}{\text{Cotton count of single yarn} \times 840} = \text{Weight in pounds of folded yarn produced per minute}$$

Example 2 Metric units and tex count

$$\frac{\text{Spindle speed (revolutions per minute)}}{\text{Number of turns of twist (turns per minute)}} = \text{Number of metres of folded yarn produced}$$

$$\frac{\text{Number of metres of folded yarn produced} \times \text{ply}}{\text{Tex count of single yarn} \times 1000} = \text{Weight in grams of folded yarn produced per minute}$$

From the weight produced per minute, as calculated above, can be calculated the weekly production:

$$\text{Weight produced per minute} \times 60 \times \text{Number of hours running} \times \text{Total number of spindles} \times \text{Efficiency}$$

The question of including a value for efficiency is important. No operation runs at 100 per cent efficiency; the twisting spindle will be stopped for filling up ends, replacing full and empty bobbins etc. Efficiency will also be influenced by the skill of the work force. Depending on circumstances, the figure could be as low as 35 per cent or as high as 90 per cent.

Calculation 3 Productivity in pirn winding

Productivity in pirn winding is controlled by three factors:

1. the rate at which the winding spindle is turned
2. the size of the pirn
3. the count or thickness of the yarn being wound.

Factors 2 and 3 control the length of yarn which the pirn will hold. In theory this could be calculated, but in practice is found by experiment as the total length can be greatly influenced by how tightly it is wound on to the pirn.

The time, in minutes, to wind a pirn may be calculated by:

$$\frac{\text{Total length of yarn contained in the pirn (yards)}}{36 \times \text{Revolutions per minute of spindle} \times \text{Circumference of pirn (inches) when half full of yarn}}$$

This calculation gives the time to wind a single pirn. It should be noted that this rate will not be true in practice as time will be required to remove full package, obtain yarn to wind, collect empty pirns etc. This influences the efficiency of the operation. For hand-wound pirns an efficiency as low as 35 per cent would not be uncommon when considered over a whole working day. This figure must therefore be taken into consideration when calculating how much can be wound during a specific period of time.

Calculation 4 Productivity of package winding (cone or cheese)

This is dependent upon two factors:

1. the speed at which the winding-on surface rotates
2. the thickness, or count, of the yarn being wound.

A typical example would be:

$$\frac{\text{RPM} \times \text{Circumference of driving surface}}{36 \times \text{Single cotton count} \times \text{Ply} \times 840} = \text{Weight in pounds produced per minute}$$

This figure can be used to calculate:

(a) the hourly or weekly production of a series of winding heads;
(b) the running time to produce a cheese or cone of a specific weight or length.

It is essential to include in this calculation a figure for efficiency. Typical efficiency figures for a modern production unit would be 80–90 per cent. Using more elementary equipment, with less well trained staff, the level of performance efficiency will be very much reduced, to a figure of about 35 per cent.

Calculation 5 Productivity of warping

The time to produce a warp may be calculated by:

$$\frac{\text{Length of warp} \times \text{Number of sections} \times \text{Efficiency}}{\text{RPM of warping mill} \times \text{Mill circumference}}$$

Note The length of the warp and warping mill circumference must be measured in the same units.

A warp must be produced carefully and accurately rather than quickly; in this instance efficiency figures are less important.

APPENDIX 2 COMPARISON OF TEX WITH OTHER COUNT SYSTEMS

English cotton count and tex

COTTON	TEX	COTTON	TEX
1	590	32	18.4
2	296	34	17.4
3	196	36	16.4
4	148	38	15.6
5	118	40	14.8
6	98.4	44	13.4
8	73.8	46	12.8
9	65.6	48	12.4
10	59	50	11.8
11	53.6	52	11.4
12	49.2	56	10.6
14	42.2	60	9.8
16	37	64	9.2
18	32.8	68	8.6
20	29.6	72	8.2
22	26.8	76	7.7
24	24.6	80	7.4
26	22.8	86	6.8
28	21	92	6.4
30	19.6	100	5.9

Woollen counts (Yorsksire skeins woolen) and tex

WOOLLEN	TEX	WOOLLEN	TEX
6	320	27	72
7	280	28	70
8	240	29	66
10	195	31	62
11	175	32	60
12	160	33	58
13	150	34	56
14	140	35	56
15	130	36	54
16	120	37	52
17	115	38	51
18	107	39	50
19	102	40	48
20	96	42	46
21	92	44	44
22	88	46	42
23	84	48	40
24	80	50	39
25	78	52	37
26	74	56	35

Metric counts and tex

METRIC	TEX	METRIC	TEX
2	500	60	16.7
4	250	64	15.6
6	167	68	14.7
8	125	72	13.9
10	100	76	13.1
12	83.3	80	12.5
14	71.4	90	11.1
16	62.5	10	10
18	55.6	110	9.1
20	50	120	8.3
24	41.7	130	7.7
28	35.7	14	7.1
32	31.3	150	6.7
36	27.8	160	6.3
40	25	170	5.9
44	22.7	180	5.6
48	20.8	190	5.3
52	19.2	200	5
56	17.9	210	4.8

INDIRECT FIXED-WEIGHT SYSTEM

English cotton count = Number of 840-yard hanks per pound

Galashiels woollen count = Number of 300-yard hanks (cuts) per 24oz

Yorkshire skeins woollen (Y.S.W.) count =
Number of 256-yard hanks per pound

Worsted count = Number of 560-yard hanks per pound

Linen count = Number of 1,000-metre hanks per kilogram

DIRECT FIXED-LENGTH SYSTEM

Tex count = Number of grams per 1,000 metres

Jute count = Number of pounds per 14,400 yards

Denier count = Number of grams per 9,000 metres

www.ingramcontent.com/pod-product-compliance
Ingram Content Group UK Ltd.
Pitfield, Milton Keynes, MK11 3LW, UK
UKHW051920300326
4997IPUK00009B/82